Forty-Two Reasons Why I Must Have a Motorcycle ... *Honey!*

Emily
Enjoy working with you -
Hope this brings a
grin!
"R. Lowent Hakes"

YOUR CHECKLIST:

- ☐ Buy this book
- ☐ Give to wife or girlfriend
- ☐ Buy motorcycle
- ☐ Live happy forever

DEDICATION:

To my wife, son and daughter for supporting
the notion that humor is vital to a healthy, happy soul.

Also, to that guy I met in the HyVee deli in Storm Lake,
Iowa many years ago (never got his name) who spied a couple
of us having breakfast in our leathers and came over to talk
motorcycles.
At one point in the conversation, I asked, "Do you ride?"
His face fell, he dropped his chin and shuffled his feet.
"No," he said quietly. "The wife."
We all knew exactly what he meant.
Buddy, this book is for you, too.

FOREWORD:

This is a book of humor based on the foibles of men and women – but mostly men.

Seriously. Any man who resorts to claiming that "God wants me to" in seeking his wife's approval to buy a motorcycle might as well tattoo "buffoon" in big block letters across his sorry butt.

And yet our sympathies are with the narrator, who appears to be a decent soul gripped by motorcycle lust. He has prepared his arguments with care, but has he overreached just a bit?

Ah, the things we do for lust.

The Reasons

1. Because I will love you more
2. I want to save my Earth
3. I already told my friends I was
      getting one so for the love of God
      don't make me back out now
4. I must have that sound
5. There is a moral imperative
6. Safer than cave diving
7. It's a better investment than RadioShack
8. It's trendy
9. Your male relatives will respect me
10. It will look awesome in the garage
11. I want to commune with Nature
12. Less expensive than a therapist
13. I'm doing it for you and the kids
14. It's good exercise for me
15. I am man; you are woman
16. Another great place to have sex
17. The neighbor kids need rides
18. I must save the economy
19. Talking to my bike will expand
      my conversational skills
20. We can use it as a Christmas tree!
21. I can't stand cages anymore
22. It will improve my vocabulary
23. Sturgis and tattoos will boost the
      buzz factor of my memoirs
24. You can't take it with you

25. It reeks of practicality
26. I could die at any moment
27. You get more alone time
28. We must change Sad Man to Happy Man
29. It's my patriotic duty
30. My manhood is at stake here
31. I could throw away my
       blood pressure medication
32. I must do it for the infrastructure
33. It will save our relationship
34. It's less expensive than golf
35. Because I don't have many toys
36. I must experience The Wave
37. I'll be able to cope with my
       'biological hankering'
38. It will help me get a raise
39. It is just so, so cool
40. I cannot live without one
41. My testicles could fall off
42. God wants me to

INTRODUCTION:

Gentlemen, I feel your pain

OK men. If you purchased this book, you may be desperate.

Your woman (wife, girlfriend, significant someone) for reasons strange and mysterious is unhappy you desire a motorcycle. Broach the subject and she looks at you as if you were Hannibal Lecter. If you stop at a dealer's showroom, she'd rather sit in the car and dig her nails into the upholstery.

God forbid a Harley should happen to roar past your house. This simple act transforms the love of your life into a grim-faced gargoyle. Her lips purse, fists clench, shoulders hunch. She pulls the drapes and cranks the volume on *House Hunters.*

At night, she secretly prays that this is all a bad dream, that this unreasonable obsession of yours will pass and that you will come to your senses. Rosary beads appear in every room, along with tiny toy motorcycles festooned with voodoo pins.

Tears, wailing and violent cursing loom around the corner. My friends, this does not bode well for you.

First and foremost, I must tell you that you have a very long row to hoe. The cliff you must scale is steep. The alligators are past your butt cheeks and climbing. Way past.

Believe me I know. I have been there.

We are the <u>victims</u> of an urgent spiritual call

My wife, God bless her, was in this state of mind some two decades ago.

I had become convinced - partially through contact with her motorcycle gear-headed brother I should point out - that there was a very real chance the wonderful world I had known for 45 odd years would crumble into granola bits if I did not get a motorcycle.

It was a sudden, urgent spiritual calling that would not abate.

So I pulled out all the stops.

I told her that Neptune would rise up from the oceans and spear me with his trident if this purchase did not come to pass. That the devil would lock me in room full of reality show contestants for eternity. That Buddha would send me back as a slug.

I believed this with all my heart, and so I pressed ahead. I met argument with argument, irrational statement with irrational statement, tear with tear. Yes, where a motorcycle is involved, a grown man can cry and often must – very easily and willfully – to try to make his point.

It was a bloody battle. It lasted for months.

When the smoke finally cleared, I found myself standing at the counter of a small Harley Davidson dealership in Cherokee, Iowa writing out a check for $15,487, plus tax. "This could mean a divorce," I told the girl behind the counter who filled out the paperwork.

"We've sold 33 bikes so far this year," she said in a deadpan voice. "Every one of those guys stood right where you are, writing the same kind of big fat check, saying the exact same thing."

As I rode home on my shiny, new 1994 Dyna Wide Glide with the two-tone aqua paint job, bobtail fender, spoked wheels, slightly ape-hung handlebars and ultra-cool forward controls which sat you back in the saddle like Peter Fonda, I experienced alternating moments of pure ecstasy and outright terror.

Yes, I was ecstatic on the bike. I knew it would save my life.

But the thought of actually rolling it into the garage at home – the home I shared with the Motorcycle Antichrist - put a pit in my stomach the size of a bowling ball. That, I feared, could be the act which ended my life.

There is a light! Go for the light!

I'm not sure how we lived through this crisis in our marriage, but we did.

Maybe when two people are so completely at odds over a serious topic within their relationship – to the point that things melt completely down to rock bottom - maybe what emerges from the ash pit is stronger than before. Maybe.

At some point, I saw a glimmer of light at the tunnel's end. The Force was with me, and I went for it. Of course it's very possible that I simply out-lasted her.

We still don't talk about it much. Occasionally, she will hop on the back of my bike for a short trip on a nice day. In return, I try to be understanding about her material wants, even though I have to admit that they often make about as much sense to me as why men have nipples. We get along, we're still in love and she no longer stares at my bike in lethal scorn every time she enters the garage.

At least I don't *think* she does.

Sometimes, however, on occasion, I have seen her open her car door a little too abruptly in the garage and come very close to nicking the fender paint on my precious bike. In those moments, I look over at her with trepidation.

"Whoops," she says.

But is there a gleam of satisfaction deep in those pretty blue eyes and possibly a slight smirk of lip?

I wonder.

Do 'this one cool thing'

The point is, I wouldn't wish the minefield path I took to get a bike on anyone. That's why I wrote this book. If I can make some other poor schmuck's perilous journey to motorcycle ownership just a bit smoother, my life might have meaning.

This book cannot work miracles, but it may help you advance your cause.

It offers evidence – some real, some imagined, some serious, some humorous – to convince your precious *woman*, that somehow there will still be a tomorrow for your marriage, your relationship, your family, your world if you can only purchase a motorcycle.

I honestly believe that could I have handed such a book to my wife 20 years ago, the battles might have been shorter, the siege less painful, the mental strain more tolerable.

She might have understood my frantic obsession just a little. She might, just might, have even grinned a time or two when she read it. When our battles over the motorcycle were in their full explosive glory, I would have paid a lot of money for even a hint of a grin.

It should be clear by now that much of the material in this book is pure tongue-in-cheek concoction, a valiant attempt to bring humor to what was once a real marital crisis. However, I have to tell you that the 13th reason titled "I'm doing it for you and the kids" actually has a basis in fact.

My son was 17 years old when I first pulled up on my gleaming Dyna Wide Glide. I love the kid, but let's just say he was a typical teenager at that time, mostly self-absorbed and not given to communicating with parents, much less complimenting them. Yet, he took one dumbfounded look at my Harley and uttered a totally profound statement I will never forget:

"Dad," he said. "This could be the *one cool thing* you have done in your life."

That single comment made it all worthwhile, and in that special moment, the seed for this book may have been sown.

So read on, biker wannabes. And have courage. Remember the words of General Omar Bradley at Normandy during WWII: *"Bravery is the capacity to perform properly even when scared half to death."*

My suggestion to you: Hand her this book and run like hell.

And then do one cool thing in your life.

                                    --- R. Lowell Hakes

THE REASONS

Reason No. 1:
Because I will love you more

Did I ever tell you I love you? Because I do. I really, really do.

And when I get my motorcycle, I will love you even more!

Because I will love *everything* more. I will love the trees and the birds and the smog and the homeless people and horse manure and parking meters and even Presidential candidates. I will love clouds and obnoxious cell phone talkers and guinea pigs and bad waiters and even hemorrhoid cream.

I will love *life* more.

And I will love *you* more because you will be *in* this wonderful life that finally having a motorcycle will create!

A life of love, and you, and horse manure and motorcycles!

Reason No. 2:

I want to save my Earth

Motorcycles get at least twice, maybe three times the gas mileage of our car or SUV, thereby saving our Earth's precious fossil fuels. They also put out fewer emissions than cars and require less metal and plastic processing for manufacturing.

This is why I must have a motorcycle.

To save my Earth.

Reason No. 3:

I already told my friends I was getting one so for the love of God don't make me back out now

It may not have been exactly the brightest thing I have ever done, but I did mention to my friends that I was getting a motorcycle.

You know, friendships are important.

Friends need to respect each other.

Do you actually expect me to go back to my friends at this point and say, "Well, I guess I can't get a motorcycle after all because my wife won't let me?" Do you have any idea how that could affect my male relationships?

I would have to move to Canada.

Do you want me to move to Canada? Eh? Eh?

Reason No. 4:

I must have that sound

I know you like certain sounds. You like to hear the gold finches chattering in the morning and the crickets chirping at night. You like the sound of a sleeping baby and the mewing of a sweet tiny kitten in your lap. You like the soft trickling burble of a mountain stream, the gentle ocean waves at dusk and the breeze rustling dry Iowa cornfields in late summer.

That is very nice.

I like certain sounds, too.

I like the jolting, throbbing, thunder-growl that belts you in the face like a big, fat two-by-four when you wake up 96 sleepy cubic inches of Road King Classic from its overnight rest in your garage. Then I like the screaming, brain-numbing windup of massive RPMs as you roar through six gears on Interstate 80 on the way to McDonald's for breakfast. Then I revel in the engine-lugging, shotgun blasts of exhaust back-offs ricocheting between nearby homes like atomic bombs as I perfect an ear-shattering deceleration down the Interstate off ramp.

See, we both like certain sounds.

Here's one sound we could both enjoy: The ticking sound of contracting metal on my exhaust pipe heat shields after a hard day's ride. We'll just stand out in the garage in silent reverence, waiting for the ticking to stop, basking in the ambiance.

Then we'll kiss and go in for dinner.

Ah, the romance of the hog.

Reason No. 5:

There is a moral imperative

If I don't get a motorcycle, I don't know how I can face myself each morning.

Morally, it's just the right thing to do.

For society, for the Universe, for me.

Reason No. 6:
Safer than cave diving

Every guy who ever tells his wife or girlfriend he needs a motorcycle gets the same response. "You'll kill yourself." Or, in my case, it was "You'll end up in a wheelchair and I refuse to take care of you."

We guys call this The Christmas Story Movie Defense, sometimes better known as You'll Shoot Your Eye Out Syndrome. It's the job of some women to worry and fret and rant over dangers real or imagined. It's the guy's job to get his BB gun in the end, or in this case, a nicely tricked-out Indian Chief Dark Horse.

According to my extensive research, here are just a few of the things that pose a greater risk for bodily injury and death than motorcycling: Smoking, sex after angioplasty, feeding sharks, sex after a stroke, breathing air in Los Angeles, sex after hernia surgery, teaching kindergarten, taking Viagra with a Jose Cuervo chaser, hitch-hiking in Juarez, walking through a mall on the day after Thanksgiving, bar-hopping with Russell Crowe or paging through Kim Kardashian's book of selfie photography.

Actually, I made that last entire paragraph up.

I once did find, however, a list of 94 "hazardous activities" on an insurance company website.

Among them were: bungee jumping, rugby, boxing, camel riding, cave diving, dragon boat racing, soccer, fruit or vegetable picking (no kidding!), go karting, gymnastics, hang gliding, hockey, kayaking, marathon running, rafting, safari trekking, snow biking, trampolining, war games (paint ball?), sky surfing, tobogganing, karate, base jumping (parachuting off a fixed structure, like a mountain or skyscraper) and abseiling (rappelling down a rock wall).

Motorcycling was not on the list.

I am not making this up.

Reason No. 7:

It's a better investment than RadioShack

A motorcycle is not a luxury toy. It's an investment. This is the absolute truth.

No matter what kind of motorcycle you get, it will hold its value well.

Buy a new Harley for $17,000. Four years later, you can sell it for $23,000!

(Actually, that is a lie. Four years later, if you keep it in good condition and put on average miles, you can probably advertise it for $15,100 and might get $14,600 or so for it. Still, the thing only cost you about $600 per year in depreciation, which is like practically getting paid to own and ride it.)

Or, buy a 15-year-old Honda Magna for $2,400. Ride the holy heck out of it for four years, then advertise it for $2,600 and the chances are some sad-eyed kid will show up at your door clutching 22 one-hundred-dollar bills he saved from his part time fast-food job. Even if you feel sorry for him and don't dicker, your net depreciation cost is only $200 or just $50 per year.

You know that SUV we have sitting in the driveway? That thing lost $4,000 in depreciation the second we crossed the curb onto the public highway in front of the dealership.

Compared to owning a car or boat or RadioShack stock, buying a motorcycle is like buying Microsoft for pennies a share.

Right now, you and I should be kicking our own butts severely for not having at least two or three motorcycles sitting in the driveway as investments!

Reason No. 8:
It's trendy

You know how you love those home and room makeovers on TV? You know how you always say how out-dated our countertops are and how we need fresh artwork for the TV room? You know how you are always looking for the latest T-shirt or yoyo or video game to get your nephews? You know how excited you were to see Capri pants back in vogue and how you are always after me to get a shirt that was designed after 1989?

Well, like it or not, the world is subject to trends. That's because people in the world *like* trends. Including you. And me.

And trends can be good things!

Like the continuing trend to buy motorcycles.

Nearly a half million new ones are sold in the U.S. every year now. That's one half million happy, trendy souls.

Make me a happy, trendy soul too!

Reason No. 9:

Your male relatives will respect me

At present, I get no respect from the males on your side of the family.

That's because when we get together, it's all golf, football and poker.

I'm a terrible golfer, the only football player I can name is Joe Montana and when it comes to poker, they read me like a large print version of Caro's *Book of Poker Tells*.

After every family gathering, my self esteem is in the toilet. I've got to beat the kids in several games of Chutes and Ladders just to be allowed back at the grownup table at Thanksgiving. At Christmas, I get self-help books instead of sports jerseys.

That will change when I pull up to your next family gathering on my 5,700 cc Boss Hoss ZZ4 – quite possibly the biggest and baddest bike on the planet.

"Uh, could we have a ride?" they will say.

"I dunno," I will reply. "I just dunno."

And then I will grin and grin.

Reason No. 10:

It will look awesome in the garage

Statistics show that the average biker gets up from his bed at least twice every night just to walk to his garage, turn on the light and gaze longingly at his motorcycle.

Why do they do this, you may ask?

Well, try to grasp what is going on here.

To motorcycle riders, the sight of a sleek, exquisite two-wheeled machine positioned silently in the garage, waiting patiently for the next ride, is akin to encountering the face of the Virgin in Michelangelo's Pieta. There is dryness in the throat, loss of speech, a quickness of pulse. The palms twitch involuntarily as if to grasp handlebars and the left foot may suffer a shift lever spasm. Occasionally, yes occasionally, there may be a tear.

That is what the mere awesomeness of a bike sitting in a garage can do.

But it's not only the fact that the bike is *there* and looking so awesome that triggers this reaction. It's the fact that the bike is *yours* for the taking. It waits solely for you. It sits in the garage emitting no sound, but you know what it wants. You can feel it. It silently prays that you will push the overhead door button, climb aboard, turn the key, grasp the clutch lever, twist the throttle and hit the starter. If you shut off the light and return to bed, you may imagine a sigh or a pouting noise coming from the garage.

I am not going so far as to say a motorcycle is a living thing.

But obviously, she has a soul.

And just the sight of her in a garage turns mortal men to mush.

Reason No. 11:

I want to commune with Nature

When we ride down the highway in our cage – excuse me – car with the windows rolled up, the air conditioning on and the kids engrossed in their *Frozen* DVD, that's not exactly communing with Nature.

When I ride down the highway on my new motorcycle, I will smell the humus of the soil as the farmer turns it over for spring planting.

I'll feel the temperature changes prickle my skin as I cruise from hilltop to valley.

I'll taste the sweet, crunchy fiber of a fresh June bug mashed against my teeth.

Life will be good because I will be one with Nature.

Can you in good faith deny me this?

Reason No. 12:

Less expensive than a therapist

Therapy: $200 per session twice a week.

That's $20,800 a year.

You can get a Victory Cross Country 8-Ball for that, smartly accessorized, and never make another shrink payment for as long as you live.

Hmmm. Lemme do the math on this one.

Reason No. 13:

I'm doing it for you and the kids

I want my family – you and the kids – to be proud of me.

But how can you be proud of someone who is not realizing his lifelong dream?

Ever since I was a boy and bought my first bicycle with my paper route money, I've been hooked on two wheels.

A boy's bike was his lifeline to the world back then – his most faithful friend and revered companion. It allowed him to earn income, cruise his neighborhood, escape his enemies and get home in time for supper. It gave him the means to run errands for his parents, give his girlfriends a lift or investigate police activity or construction projects way on the other side of town which would have been too far to walk.

Most importantly, a boy developed a skill that translated into pure fun. He could ride like the wind, steer on a dime, hop obstacles and coast "no-handed" down hills. Like the cowboy and horse before him, the bike became an extension of his own body.

And even though motorcycles were few and far between in that era, his adult goal was always to have one. He watched movies like *Easy Rider,* adored *CHiPS* on TV and revered Evel Knievel. He attached playing cards to his spokes with clothes pins, and even though it made pedaling exhausting, he felt the sound it produced put him that much closer to his dream.

I have this dream. Always have had it.

Let me reach it. Please. It would crush me to let you and the kids down.

Reason No. 14:

It's good exercise for me

Like any sport, motorcycle riding burns calories. Some examples:

- Grunting into too-tight leather vest and chaps – 500 calories
- Steering, shifting and braking for two hours – 300 calories
- Polishing fenders, chrome and tires - 200 calories
- Strutting through parking lots and music festivals - 400 calories
- Lifting beers at biker bars - 600 calories
- Dancing with wild babes at biker bars – 1,200 calories
- Rushing to the bathroom at biker bars - 300 calories

Reason No. 15:

I am man; you are woman

I recognize that you *need* things. You need stuff like expensive makeup, pilates class, fashionable shoes and Girls Night Out at the wine bar. And you need to *do* things. Like enroll the kids in too many outside activities and replace perfectly good furniture with similar furniture, but new.

Well, you need to understand that I *need* things, too.

I need a motorcycle.

And I need to *do* things, too.

I need to ride a motorcycle.

You are woman. I am man.

We both need stuff and we need to do stuff.

It's not always the same stuff.

And that's OK!

Reason No. 16:
Another great place to have sex

This one is a bit touchy.

Now I know for a fact that people have sex on motorcycles. After all, I am not a complete dolt and I do have a computer which is hooked up to the World Wide Web.

Just how these people accomplish this is where things get a little iffy. In other words, it certainly *looks* like they are having fun and have figured out certain techniques and positioning methods that make the whole process appear to be a comfortable and pleasurable way to enjoy each other's love.

And although I certainly support ranking the motorcycle extremely high as a place to have sex – right up there with the hot tub, kitchen counter and the No. 8 green at Pebble Beach – my fear is that a certain amount of athleticism may be required to complete the task.

The whole point is that just the *thought* of a sleek, shiny, testosterone-reeking machine just sitting in the garage waiting for couples interested in coupling has tremendous appeal.

I'm not saying we could test it out the first night I bring the bike home, but maybe after a couple of aerobics classes and some Tai Chi, who knows!

I think maybe we should practice while the bike is standing still, however.

At least at first.

Reason No. 17:

The neighbor kids need rides

I must tell you, for years I have felt bad that the neighbors have done so many nice things for us and I have been unable to reciprocate.

Remember when Kevin on the south side helped me replace the guts in the upstairs toilet when it wouldn't stop running? Duane always drives his snow blower down our main sidewalk and even old Barton out back has given me more tomatoes and growing tips than I deserve.

With a motorcycle, I would give rides to their kids and grandkids every Saturday morning. Kids love loud machines and I would be like the beloved Pied Piper of the neighborhood. You would look out the window, watch me load up another tyke for a safe, low-speed cruise around the block and think how happy the kids look and what nice neighbors we are.

And what a wonderful, kind, caring, giving husband you have.

And you would smile!

Reason No. 18:

I must save the economy

My country's economy needs me to buy a motorcycle.

Times are not so great. We've got an emerging China, constant layoffs here at home, immigrants driving down wages and the Walton kids continuing to run around steamrolling Ma and Pa stores into the dust.

I must do my part. If by buying a motorcycle I can keep one more U.S. motorcycle salesman in groceries for just one more week; if I can keep the doors of J & P Cycles Motorcycle Parts open for just another day; if I can keep the Harley Davidson line workers in York, Pennsylvania in Ding Dongs for just one more coffee break…well, it would all be worth it.

Reason No. 19:

Talking to my bike will expand my conversational skills

This is a little known fact: Men talk to their motorcycles.

In fact, men often have very long conversations with their motorcycles.

They will never admit it and you will never witness the conversation. It happens when they are alone with their bikes in the garage, or rolling down a lonely stretch of highway or stopping along a roadside to gaze at the scenery.

Some examples of conversation:

■ In the garage: (softly) "How are you doing, baby? You got enough oil? Tire pressure OK? Here, let me wipe down that fender a bit. How's that? Does that feel goooooood? You wanna go out tomorrow? Huh? Do you? Should we go for a little spin?"

■ On the highway: (screamed, with feeling) "Yeeeeehawwwwww! Go baby! Go baby! Yes! Yes! Talk to me! Talk to me! Who's your Daddy? Huh? Who's your Daddy?"

■ Parked at a scenic overlook: (mellow) "Look at that. You ever seen anything like that? Man, that is gorgeous. Just look. Can you see it? Ok, you ready to move on? You want to move on down the road? OK, here we go now. We'll take it slow so you can look."

For most men, it is just normal conversation, like you might have with a good friend or even an intimate lover. I've been told that some men slip into baby talk from time to time with their bikes, but I think that probably should be avoided. ("Daddy's widdo baby girl wanna go weal weal fast? Baby wanna see da mountain? Oooooh! Wookit da biiiig twuck!")

The thing is, you say you want me to be more verbal and share my feelings, so why don't we seize this opportunity to expand my conversational skills by getting a motorcycle?

It really only makes sense.

Reason No. 20:

We can use it
as a Christmas tree!

Hard-core bikers in northern climates often bring their motorcycles into the living room for winter storage.

Here they can keep it warm and safe and hop on for a pretend ride from time to time when the snow drifts outside make biking impossible.

The best part about this is that you can hang ornaments all over the handlebars and make it your Christmas tree!

Just think of it! No more having to trudge out into the snow trailing whining kids, hack down a young spruce in the prime of life, drag it back home and then feel guilt all December for contributing to more ozone depletion.

It's a win-win!

Reason No. 21:
I can't stand cages anymore

Cars are cages. There's no getting past it.

You cruise along in a hermetically-sealed plastic tube of safety glass with wheels. You breathe temperature and humidity-controlled recycled air, listen to acoustically precise music and recline in heated, lumbar-supported leather seats surrounded by a state-of-the-art crash-resistant steel frame and fluffy pillow airbags.

The world outside passes by like a continuous roll of painted scenery held up to the car windows by circus attendants. Sometimes it's difficult to determine if you are riding in your car or sitting in your living room watching the Travel Channel.

On a motorcycle, you are not an observer of the landscape. You *are* the landscape.

Your senses revel in the rush of air, the smells, the sounds and the sights bombarding you as you plummet over the highway – more vulnerable to the environment, yes, but more alive!

Cages have their moments, it is true.

But given a choice?

Give me a bike.

It will improve my vocabulary

Just think of the brand new mind-expanding vocabulary I will learn by hanging around motorcycle enthusiasts, who are well-known as some of the most eloquent bipeds on the planet.

Some examples:

Yard Sharks – dogs that run out of nowhere to bite at your tires

Buffler – severe leg burn from a hot muffler (all real bikers have at least one)

Desmodronic - a Ducati-designed valve opening and closing system that does not rely on springs

Nipple Surfing – flying off the motorcycle chest down on the pavement

Waxer - a guy who would rather wax his bike than ride it

Wingabago - a Honda Gold Wing with all the extras

Long Bike - a chopper with long forks and stretched-out back

Centrifugal Inertia - the phenomenon that increases the stability of the bike the faster the wheels turn

Bagger - motorcycle with hard or soft saddlebags and possibly additional storage to accommodate some serious long-distance riding

Protein Facial - what you get riding without a wind screen

Kwak - a Kawasaki (pronounced "quack")

Trailer Trash - riders who trailer their bike further than they ride it

Skid Lid - helmet

Truck Suck - severe semi trailer truck turbulence

SQUID - Stupidly Quick, Underdressed, Imminently Dead. A reckless, inexperienced rider without proper equipment and attire, riding beyond his ability and endangering all he encounters

Chromosexual – one who is severely addicted to continually adding more chrome to his bike, well beyond any reasonable usefulness or aesthetic purpose

Poser - rides only to impress. May not even like motorcycles

Sleeper - a bike that looks slow, but is a screamer

Purple Hooters - a topless female rider in cold weather

Wouldn't you be proud to have a husband with a classy vocabulary like this?

Reason No. 23:

Sturgis and tattoos will boost the buzz factor of my memoirs

If I wrote my memoirs today, I'd have to title the book *My Button-Downed Life.*

The closest I have ever been to letting it all hang out was at my cousin's bar mitzvah in 1988 when I jumped into the pool with my loafers on. The artificial inseminator guy at a turkey farm has a more exciting life than mine.

Sturgis and a couple of tattoos could change all of that.

You've probably heard about Sturgis, that tiny town near the Black Hills of South Dakota that swells with nearly one half million motorcycles during a gigantic rally in the early part of August each year.

It's the Mecca for motorcycle social energy, with an enlightening experience at every turn, mostly based on the sacred "three Bs" of the iron horse culture: Beer, Bands and Boobs. Outlandish material for memoirs is practically guaranteed.

But to please you, I'll carefully train for the trip.

To begin with, I'll quit shaving, drink a case of Schlitz every night and lock myself in the basement watching vintage "Girls Gone Wild" videos. That will provide a good foundation.

During the final weeks before the rally, you can help simulate the lengthy motorcycle journey across the vast South Dakota prairie by whacking me on the butt with a tire iron for about an hour every night.

Together, we'll make sure I'm ready. We are a team!

And, of course, I'll need a tattoo.

I have dreamed about a tattoo of a beautiful naked woman with a face a lot like yours. She's positioned like a goddess over my heart, a banner with your name on it draped modestly but artistically over her most private regions. Flowers bloom about her feet, each with the face of one of our children in the center of the petals. Behind her is our house, with your parents waving from the windows like the sweet old grandparents they are.

This is what I dream of: A beautiful tattoo over my heart which would constantly remind me of you and our delightful family and the wonderful life we all have together, a life enriched through my entry into the motorcycle culture to boost the buzz factor of my memoirs.

On the other hand, a tattoo would hurt a lot.

So forget it.

Reason No. 24:
You can't take it with you

A lot of people have tried, but it's really true that you can't take it with you.

That's because nobody knows exactly when they are going to leave this glorious Earth. If we did know, we still might not be able to take it with us, but by God we could go a long way toward making sure we spent most of it before we left!

The point is, you *can't* take it with you. And if you can't, that means you've got to uncork a little fun, cut loose from the tether and spend some of that hard-earned cash while you still have enough coordination to plunge one hand into your pocket and dig out your Visa card.

What a tragedy, to think a guy would slave away his entire life yearning for that day when he felt financially comfortable enough to buy himself a heck of a nice motorcycle, only to never reach that day!

I want to reach that day. I *need* to reach that day.

And the sooner the better.

Reason No. 25:

It reeks of practicality

It's true. There are few more practical and efficient modes of transportation than the motorcycle.

Why do you think the Chinese, French and Italians ride them everywhere they go?

Fantastic gas mileage, low maintenance, easy cleaning, long life, reasonable insurance costs, holds its value – and the ability to always find a parking spot no matter how crowded your destination is with "cages."

Throw in the fun factor as a bonus and you've got one extra fine bargain of a machine.

What's that smell?

It's the sweet reek of practicality and it comes from every motorcycle we meet!

Reason No. 26:

I could die at any moment

You know at my age, I don't buy concert tickets very far in advance.

I could be stricken flat at any moment, lay in a hospital bed like a carrot for three months, then you pull the plug and it's over.

People at my funeral would say: "A tragedy. He never got that motorcycle he always wanted, did he?"

Of course by that time, it won't make much difference to me. I'm gone.

But for you to have to live on knowing that?

Oh, the horror! The horror!

Reason No. 27:
You get more alone time

Let's be honest.

There was a time when we wanted to do everything together. We were newlyweds, hand-holders and skating rink smoochers. We made out in movies and stared at each other across malt shop tables like Lady and the Tramp.

I'm not saying those days are gone. We still have the fire.

But when you throw kids and mortgages and busy jobs and the hustles and hassles of grinding out a life into the mix, we must face the reality that each of us enjoys our "alone time" more these days than we did earlier in the marriage.

With a motorcycle in the family, you'll have a little more peace and quiet to yourself. I'll still be there when you need me, or the kids need me, or Grandma, or the soccer team. But when the weather's right and the road beckons, I can be gone and you can take a day with your friends, or browse the bargain book section at Barnes & Noble, or chill at the matinee.

Just think of it! Both of us, in love, but basking in alone time – with no guilt!

Reason No. 28:

We must change
Sad Man to Happy Man

You always say I am cheerful. You think that I am Happy Man.

Well, although I often pretend to be, I am actually *not* Happy Man.

I am Sad Man.

Sad Man drives around town in his Dodge Caravan, sighing softly to himself when he passes a house where a guy has placed his 1,854 cc Yamaha Stratoliner Midnight in the yard with a for sale sign on it. Sad Man wants to stop and look, but he can't because the significant someone in his life hates motorcycles and he knows it is no use.

Sad Man pulls up to a stop light and four couples on Ultra Classic Electra Glides thunder up beside him, laughing and grinning. When the light changes, they are off in a roar of smoke. Sad Man sinks a little lower behind the steering wheel of his van.

Sad Man passes a local pub where a dozen spit-shined bikes of varying brands have been carefully backed up to the curb. Intermittent bursts of merriment flow from the bar's open door. He imagines friendly people in black T-shirts embroidered with slogans of questionable taste sitting at tables drinking Coronas and Jack Daniels, regaling each other with adventures of the road – the priceless tales of past journeys and excited talk of trips to come.

Sad Man picks up the pizza his wife has ordered, but on the way home, pulls over to the side of the road, turns off the van's ignition and weeps quietly. His wife will never even notice the tear stains on the cardboard box which holds her thin-crust Vegetarian Supreme.

You have the power.

You can change Sad Man into Happy Man.

Use your power…for the good of mankind.

I beg you.

Reason No. 29:

It's my patriotic duty

What could be more American than cruising down the interstate some hot July afternoon on a 1600 cc six-speed Dyna Street Bob with Screaming Eagle pipes, fringed leather bags, a custom tombstone taillight and Old Glory flying from the sissy bar?

Nothing.

My manhood is at stake here

Men do certain things today that are, well, *manly* things.

Things like hunting elk or bull riding or pummeling other men inside roped-off areas surrounded by fanatics screaming for blood.

It's been that way for eons. Even a couple of thousand years ago, men were racing chariots, fighting tigers bare-handed and throwing boiling tar at each other for the fun of it – surrounded even then by, yes, those early fanatics screaming for blood.

Somehow, motorcycles became linked to man's continuing desire to let his testosterone run wild. It must connect somehow to speed, power, noise, risk, balance, skill – all of that stuff that gives a man the feeling that he is doing something wicked and dangerous, even if he is only riding to the 7-Eleven for olive loaf.

Sure, I could *not* get a motorcycle. I could keep tooling around town in my fake-wood-sided mini-van and waste my days trying to keep my five iron from slicing into the trees. I could spend my vacations gazing at the Rockies from an air-conditioned Amtrak observation car. I could cower in the dark, giggling at *Seinfeld* reruns while a perfectly fine stretch of lonely curving blacktop road cries out for the wheels of a 1099 cc Shadow Sabre.

But would I still be a man?

Not bloody likely!

Reason No. 31:

I could throw away my blood pressure medication

A lot of things can calm a guy down.

Sticking your bare feet in warm Jell-O.

Napping naked in the grass on the front lawn.

Listening to Ben Stein read *War and Peace* on audio tape.

But give me a big bike, blue sky and sweet green cornfields on either side of a winding blacktop road any day. If true peace comes from getting in touch with your inner soul, then riding a sleek iron horse is about as close to that core as you can get.

Even a one-hour journey leaves you refreshed, relaxed and ready to return to the grind.

One hour in Nirvana is all it takes.

One hour.

Reason No. 32:
I must do it for the infrastructure

America's infrastructure – railroads, bridges and especially highways – are in bad shape.

Our heavy semi trucks, giant motor homes and even SUVs are chewing up asphalt and concrete like Godzilla in Times Square.

A motorcycle, with less than one-half the tire surface imprint of your average car and one-fourth the weight, is like a delicate sand bug flitting over the beach and hardly disturbing a grain. If we all drove motorcycles, the Interstate highways could quadruple their life spans.

I must do my part to save the infrastructure.

I must.

It will save our relationship

My getting a motorcycle could save our relationship.

(Now right this minute, I am getting vibrations that you may not actually believe this. You may be rolling your eyes back into their sockets, or you may be getting ready to fling this book into the microwave. Wait! Hear me out.)

You see, it is not good for woman and man to go through life in a cohabitated state and never have an argument. We have all seen these kinds of relationships and reacted with disgust.

"Look at how he pulls her chair back for her. Who is he – Sir Francis Drake?"

"Look how she laughs at his jokes when she secretly wants to slice his guts open."

"My God! They actually kissed goodbye! Take me to the barfatorium!"

Men and women in complacent, seemingly flawless relationships with no lip-biting, fist-clenching or raised voices set themselves up for big trouble down the road. Years of pent-up antagonism eventually take their toll. Things may appear to be rolling along smoothly, then at their 50th anniversary banquet, she jams a cake fork into his throat.

By buying this motorcycle, I will actually ensure that we will be a normal couple. We will have a healthy and active argument topic which can last us for several years. No phony-baloney pretending to be in a perfect relationship for us!

You'll be able to bash me almost daily about this expensive, dangerous and impractical purchase I have made – your words - and our relationship will thrive and grow and last!

(Don't thank me. In a good relationship, making a grand effort to save it means never having to say thank you.)

Reason No. 34:

It's less expensive than golf

Cost of golf for 20 years: $5,000 initiation fee, $2,000 per year dues; $1,200 per year clubhouse dining account; $2,500 total to buy new set of clubs every five years; $3,000 per year bar bill and gambling losses on course; $500 per year clothing and accessories; $2,000 per year trips to other golfing destinations with The Boys.

Total golf costs for 20 years: $181,500

Cost of motorcycle for 20 years: $15,000 to purchase bike; $2,000 for accessories; $1,000 for leathers; $600 per year fuel costs; $700 per year maintenance and insurance; $5,000 one-time fee to upgrade to new bike after ten years; $2,000 per year liquor, lodging and motorcycle rally fees.

Total motorcycle costs for 20 years: $89,000

Bottom line: Motorcycles are half the cost of golf and six times more fun!

Reason No. 35:

Because I don't have many toys

Scoff if you will, but I do not have many toys.

Oh sure, maybe a big screen TV.

And a fishing boat.

And some computer games.

But those are things you like, too, and the kids. Those are more *family type* things.

Ever since I was a little kid, I have had to share my toys with my siblings. Every Christmas, whether it was an Erector Set or Lincoln Logs or a Lionel Train, I'd have to allow my brothers to play with my stuff until it was lost or wrecked or just failed to work anymore.

The way I see it, I'm overdue for a nice big toy for me.

Just me.

All mine.

It'll be MY motorcycle. MINE!

(But of course, you can ride it whenever you want!)

Reason No. 36:

I must experience The Wave

I'm not sure you know this, but the day you purchase a motorcycle you automatically become a member of a congenial fraternity.

There are no annual fees. There is no Hell Week initiation. Nobody is black-balled. You will only know the names of a handful of its members. Thousands of others you will see on the road, but never meet in person.

To become a member of this unique fraternity, just get on a bike and roll down the road. The Wave tells you that you are "in" before you have gone five miles.

What is The Wave you ask?

The Wave is the small, silent courtesy greeting bikers extend to each other when they meet traveling opposite directions on a two-lane highway.

Some raise a hand in a conventional wave. Some point a finger at the pavement or at your bike wheels. Some give the two-fingered "V" (for victory or V-twin) sign. Some just let their hands float gently on the rushing air as if they were preparing to play the piano.

How did it start? Nobody knows.

What does it mean? Many things.

It speaks volumes.

In a nutshell, The Wave says this:

We are brothers and sisters, you and I. We and only we know what it is like to be out here on the road, basking in the freedom and the danger of open air riding, sometimes fighting the elements of Nature and sometimes the nature of humanity.

We share the bond of thundering down this glorious highway and roaring across this precious nation, joyful in our pursuit of the next curve, the next mountain, the next lake, the next prairie, the next little town.

We are happy to share the road with our caged friends, but to us, they are only friends. Those on two wheels will always be more -- our brothers and our sisters -- and we wave to say we share your pain, your pleasure and your spirit of life regardless of who you are or what you ride.

Could there ever be a more fantastic club?
I must join.

I'll be able to cope with my 'biological hankering'

A terrible thing happens to men about my age. They go a little nutty.

They start thinking about things. Things like why do we exist? What lies beyond the edge of the Universe? Why won't that damn kid of mine quit texting and pay attention?

The questioning, the sudden irritability, the loss of faith, the night sweats. These are all classic symptoms.

It's biological, really. Call it male menopause. Call it temporary insanity. Call it what you want. It can't be helped.

The sad part is that pretty soon these menopausal men get a *hankering* for stuff. Some of it can be pretty serious hankering. Like hankering for a yacht for a trip to Australia, hankering to live in Nepal with the monks or hankering for a breast-augmented trophy wife with a trust fund.

Fortunately, for about 75 percent of men, the ailment is less severe and becomes focused on hankering their way into getting a motorcycle.

That's where I am right now. I'm in mid-hanker for a motorcycle.

The good news is that even though it's biological and can't be helped, my particular fixation is a lot better than most of the alternatives. I mean really. Do you want to huddle with me in a parka in Kathmandu for the rest of your life?

So really, you should be *celebrating* this hanker!

Let's break out the Cold Duck!

Reason No. 38:

It will help me get a raise

How, you may ask? Two ways.

First off, motorcycling builds confidence. If you can thread between semis on the New Jersey Turnpike at 80 miles an hour on a Kawasaki Vulcan 1600 Mean Streak, you can handle just about any project thrown your way at work.

Second, people immediately take notice if they know you ride. Their admiration and respect blossoms. Bosses, if they are male at least, and some female bosses as well, sit up a notch upon securing that information. If they ride, they immediately forge a new bond with you. If they don't ride, they still want to and want to get closer to a guy who does.

My best guess is that one year after securing my motorcycle, I'll have enough raises under my belt to cover the full purchase price.

You think I'm joking?

You don't know Corporate America!

Reason No. 39:

It is just so, so cool

The blessed reality is that a motorcycle is just about the coolest thing ever created by man or God. Yet for some reason, some wives and girlfriends have a hard time grasping that fact.

Perhaps this little analogy can help:

Right now, if I go to Hardware Hank for some window caulk, I enter the garage, get behind the wheel of our 12-year-old mini-van and complete a totally boring and uneventful drive to the store. Once there, I am just like every other Saturday guy in faded khakis and a varnish-stained polo shirt picking up supplies for his weekend chores. Nobody looks twice.

Now with a motorcycle, this trip becomes an entirely different experience because my "coolness quotient" has spiked.

Here's what I see happening:

As you rumble out of the garage, every neighbor kid and his hedge-clipping father give you the high sign. At stop lights, every driver and passenger nod in admiration.

When you thunder up to the store, the heads of six pert young women sipping lattes and clicking on laptops in the Starbucks window next door turn your way – some even stopping conversations with boyfriends in mid-sentence. What they see is a guy in dark glasses, a black T-shirt, faded jeans and harness boots masterfully backing his throaty hog to the curb, swinging a leg over, propping his helmet on the sissy bar and sauntering into the store.

The store's greeter, who once owned a Suzuki when he was in the Army, wants to talk bikes for a while, so you do. Checking out with the caulk, the pimple-faced cash register kid gives a "nice ride" thumbs up. Back at the curb, a young couple has stopped to admire your Bassani Road Rage pipes, the guy nearly vomitous with envy and his squeeze softly consoling him with love murmurs and promises she will never keep.

You fire the bike back up, and the six heads in Starbucks snap for a second time, and you feel twelve eyes upon your bad back tire as you exit the parking lot. Or maybe those eyes are on your butt, who knows?

And this is the way it is. Everywhere you go.

You are constantly in the public focus, a continuous one-person parade.

Nothing else gives you this coolness factor. Not cars, not clothes, not even plastic surgery.

Nobody can explain it.

It's just . . . the motorcycle.

It is just so, so cool.

I cannot live without one

If I cannot have a motorcycle, I may as well not live. You might as well just smother me with a pillow in my sleep. You might as well take that sharp, eight-pronged comb you mess with from time to time and jab it straight into my eyes.

If I can't have a motorcycle, you might as well stick my hands in the blender and churn away until my fingers are nubbins. What use are they if they can't curl around the handlebars of a pulsating, 2,300 cc Triumph Rocket III?

If I can't have a motorcycle, you might as well just push me down the basement steps. Make sure I hit head first and that my neck snaps cleanly. I'd want to go quickly.

The insurance is paid up, so go ahead. I'll be going to a better place.

There must be hundreds of Harleys in Heaven.

Reason No. 41:

My testicles could fall off

It is true that this happened once to a guy.

His name was Jerome Snodwell and he lived in New Jersey. He tried for five years to get his wife's permission to get a motorcycle and he finally gave up.

A year later, he was standing at the counter in Panera Bread munching a whole grain baguette and *doink*, his testicles fell off. A clerk raced over and put them in an insulated to-go coffee cup packed with ice and they rushed him to the hospital, but it was too late.

Poor Jerry.

Do you want this to happen to me?

Do you? Do you?

Reason No. 42:

God wants me to

Ok. You may not believe this, but it is absolutely true. God spoke to me.

He wants me to have a motorcycle.

I was in the shower last Tuesday. He appeared through the fog and mist.

He looked as you might expect. Caucasian, flowing white robe, ZZ Top beard, John Lennon glasses, long white hair.

But he wore a red bandanna and black biker boots.

"I just got back from Sturgis," he said. "Things are hoppin' out there. Pretty cool."

"You ride?" I said.

"Of course!" he replied. "Who do you think told William Harley to try making a cylinder out of a tomato soup can back in 1901?"

I hoped he'd get to the point of his visit. It was a little uncomfortable being naked in front of God. But then if you think about it, I guess all of us are that way all the time anyway.

"Frankly, you need a motorcycle," he said. "Your soul will not be complete until you have one. If the obsession doesn't kill you, your wife will, or I will. The best choice for all concerned is to just let you have your way."

"Can you make it happen?" I pleaded.

"I can," he said. "But I won't."

I lost it then. Fell to my knees.

"Help me, God!" I blubbered. "Help me!"

"Quit blubbering," he said. "She's *your* woman. You deal with it. I've got my own problems. Jonathan Winters and Joan Rivers are still stuck in Processing and all Hell is breaking loose down there."

And then he was gone.

But the message was clear.

God wants me to have a motorcycle.

And Honey, we just can't fight the will of God.

Acknowledgements:

My thanks to Joan Hakes, Anthony Hakes, Molly Hakes, Nancy Hakes, Craig Fratzke, Tony Craine and Tim Sorensen.

Also, special thanks to Dennis Fitzgerald and Big Rich Kneifl, motorcycle mentors whose passion for two-wheeled travel was highly contagious.